MEMORIAL

OF

EDWARD D. NEILL,

PRAYING

The publication of the records of the Virginia Company, of London, now in the library of Congress.

MAY 28, 1868.—Referred to the Committee on the Library and ordered to be printed.

To the Senate and House of Representatives of the United States of America in Congress assembled:

While historians have made diligent search in the state paper office of Great Britain for documents illustrative of the early colonization of the territory comprised within the limits of the United States of America, they appear to have overlooked the most valuable manuscripts of that period, in the Library of Congress, which are the minutes and transactions of the great London corporation, known as the Virginia Company, from the year 1619 to its dissolution, and written out by their own secretaries.

The memorialist, while preparing for publication a little book called Terra Mariœ, or Threads of Maryland Colonial History, made himself familiar with the obsolete chirography and interesting contents of these records, and proposes, without pecuniary compensation, to annotate and prepare the manuscripts for publication, under the direction of the Librarian of Congress, provided he is authorized to employ two copyists, each at $80 per month, for a period not exceeding twelve months, and has a small sum appropriated for necessary stationery and contingent expenses.

The records, if printed, would form two octavo volumes of about 500 pages each. The appended extracts will give some idea of the varied contents of these records. To those who may think the labor would be unnecessary, I can only quote a sentence from the letter of Governor Dudley of Massachusetts, written in 1630, to the Countess of Lincoln:

> If any tax me for wasting paper with recording these small matters, such may consider that small things, in the beginning of natural or politic bodies, are as remarkable as greater in bodies full grown.

All which is respectfully submitted.

EDWARD D. NEILL.

MAY 26, 1868.

EXTRACTS FROM THE MANUSCRIPT RECORDS OF THE VIRGINIA COMPANY OF LONDON.

PATENT FOR THE LEYDEN PURITANS.

May 26, 1619.—"One Mr. Wyncop* commended to the company by the Earl of Lincoln†, intending to go in person to Virginia, and there to plant himself and his associates, presented his patent now to the court, which was referred to the committee that meeteth upon Friday morning at Mr. Treasurer's house, to consider, and if need be, to correct the same."

June 17, 1619.—"By reason it grew late, and the court ready to break up, and as yet Mr. John Whincop's‡ patent for him and his associates to be read, it was ordered that the seal should be annexed unto it,§ and referred the trust thereof to the auditors, to examine that it agree with original, which if it does not, they have permission to bring it into the court and cancel it."

February 2, 1619, old style.‖—A grant of land to "John Peirce¶ and his associates, their heirs and assigns."

"It was ordered allso,** by generale consent, that such captaines or leaders of particularr plantations that shall go there to inhabite by virtue of their grants, and plant themselves, their tenants, and servants in Virginia, shall have liberty, till a forme of government be there settled them, of associatinge unto them divers of the gravest and discreetest of their companies, to make orders, ordinances, and constitutions for the better orderinge and dyrectinge of their servants and busines, provided they be not repugnant to the lawes of England." ††

February 16, 1619, old style.‡‡—"Whereas, at the last court a special committee was appointed for the managing of the £500 given by an unknown person for educating the infidels' children, Mr. Treasurer signified that they have met and taken into consideration the proposition of Sir John Wolstenholme,§§

* Palfrey, in his accurate History of New England, quoting Bradford, says the patent of the Leyden people was "not taken in the name of any of their own company, but in the name of Mr. John Wincob, a religious gentleman then belonging to the Countess of Lincoln, who intended to go with them."

† Thomas Clinton, Earl of Lincoln, had three daughters—Frances, the wife of John, a son of Sir Ferdinando Gorges; Susan, the wife of John Humphrey, first deputy governor of Massachusetts bay; Arbella, the wife of Isaac Johnson, one of the settlers of Salem, Massachusetts. The ship Arbella, which landed Winthrop and company at Salem, was so named in compliment to Lady Arbella.

‡ In the records this name is also written Wyncopp. Our histories spell it Wencob. Bradford, speaking of Wyncopp, says, "God so disposed, as he never went."

§ The date of this patent has hitherto been unknown to historians. (Palfrey, volume 1, p. 154.) Bradford in History of New Plymouth, says, "This being sent over for them (at Leyden) to consider."

‖ In England the new year commenced on March 25 until 1752, when the Gregorian or New Style was adopted.

¶ John Peirce and other traders of London appear to have made a contract with the Leyden people and furnished them with transportation to, and subsistence, after reaching the coast of America, and two or three months before the sailing of the colonists of the Mayflower, endeavored to have intrusted to them a fund given to the Virginia Company for the education of Indian children.

** In this extract the spelling of the manuscript is retained.

†† By permission of the Virginia Company, the first representative and legislative assembly in America had met on July 30, 1619, at Jamestown, and Sir Edwin Sandys and associates were ready to concede to the people of the proposed new plantation the liberty of framing their own laws.

‡‡ The germs of republican liberty were brought with the emigrants from the old world and rapidly grew in the new settlements.

§§ Sir John Wolstenholme was a prominent London merchant, with whom Brewster, Cushman, and others of the Leyden people had correspondence.

He had assisted in settling Kent isle, in the Chesapeake, before Baltimore obtained his patent for Maryland. At his sole expense, in 1632 he built a church at Stanmore, near London, and after his death, at the age of 77 years, was, on November 25, 1639, there buried.

that John Peirce and his associates might have the training and bringing up of some of these children; but the said committee, for divers reasons, think it inconvenient; first, because they intend not to go this two or three months, and then, after their arrival will be long in settling themselves; as also, that the Indians are not acquainted with them, and so they may stay four or five years before they have account that any good is done."

July 16, 1621.—"It was moved, seeing that Mr. John Peirce had taken a patent of Sir Ferdinando Gorges, and thereupon seated his company within limits of the northern plantations, as by some was supposed, whereby he seemed to relinquish the benefit of the patent he took of this company, that therefore the said patent might be called in, unless it might appear he would begin to plant within the limits of the southern colony."*

DISPUTE OF NORTH AND SOUTH COLONY.

March 15, 1619, old style —Sir Edwin Sandys said: "That the north colony intending to re-plant themselves in Virginia, had petitioned to the king and to the lords for the obtaining a new patent, which the lords referred unto the Lord Duke and the Lord of Arundel. And the Lord Arundel delivered it to him for to call the council, understanding of some differences about fishing betwixt them, and that if they could not determine on it, that then to return their opinions to their lordships, whereupon, accordingly having met, and, as formerly, disputed the business, they could not conclude thereof, but dissented the one from the other, that therefore, according to his lordship's command, the court would please to nominate some to give intelligence how the business betwixt them doth depend, which the court, perceiving not to understand the cause so well as himself, most earnestly besought him to take the pains, which he being very loth and unwilling, by reason of the exceeding multitude of the company's business depending upon him, desired to be excused; but not prevailing, he was so earnestly solicited thereunto, he could not gainsay it, whereupon they associated unto him Sir John

* Palfrey and others appear to think that the original destination of the Mayflower was to the territory of the London Company or southern colony. But the above minute of this company shows that Peirce had been in the interest of Gorges and others, proprietors of the northern colony. In the compact of government drawn up in the cabin of the Mayflower, and signed November 11, 1620, the passengers state that they have undertaken "a voyage to plant the first colony in the northern part of Virginia."

The records of the Virginia Company agree with the statement of Morton, who says that they "obtained letters patent, for the northern part of Virginia, of King James of famous memory." Governor Dudley also stated in 1630, "They, of Plymouth, came with patents from King James, and have since obtained others."

An examination of the patent granted by the council of New England, on June 1, 1621, shows that there had been an arrangement with John Peirce; the agreement is "between the president and council of New England, of the one party, and John Peirce, citizen and cloth-worker of London, and his associates of the other party, witnesseth, that whereas, the said John Peirce and his associates, have already transported, and undertaken to transport, at their cost and charges, themselves and divers persons into New England." (Massachusetts Historical Society Collections; fourth series, volume 2.)

Weston also, on July 6, 1621, writes from London, "We have procured you a charter which is better than your former, and with less limitation." (Bradford's New Plymouth.)

Gorges and associates succeeded, on July 23, 1620, in having a warrant from King James directed to the proper officer, ordering a new patent to be sealed for the northern colony, although until November 3 the seal was not affixed. Bradford, in allusion to the strife to secure the Puritan colonists, remarks: "About this time they had heard, by Mr. Weston and others, that sundry honorable lords had obtained a large grant from the King for the more northerly part of that country, distinct from the Virginia patent, and wholly secluded from Virginia government, to be called by another name, viz: New England. Unto which Mr. Weston and the chiefest of them began to incline, thinking it was best for them to go to, as for other reasons, chiefly for the hope of present profit to be made by fishing. But in all business the acting part is most difficult, especially when the work of many agents must concur. So it was found in them, for some of them who should have gone, in England, fell off and would not go. Other merchants and friends that had offered to adventure the money withdrew and pretended many excuses. Some, disliking, went to Guiana; others, again, would

Danvers, Mr. Harbert, and Mr. Keightley to report thereon to-morrow morning at 8 of the clock."*

May 11, 1620.—"Forasmuch as the north colony hath petitioned to the king for obtaining a new patent, and therein to declare the one colony to have privileges within the other, this company finding themselves grieved thereby, being a means to debar them from the immunities, his Majesty hath freely and graciously granted them for matter of fishing, it is agreed that a petition likewise be exhibited to his Majesty for this company."

November 4, 1620.—Sir Edwin Sandys remarked: "That he was informed that Sir Ferdinando Gorges had procured unto himself and others a new patent (now passed his Majesty's great seal) wherein certain words were conveyed that did not only contradict a former order of the lords of the counsel, which the lords, after a full hearing of the allegations on both sides, had set down in June last, by which this company had yielded some of their right to do them good, had thereby promised to fish only for their necessities and transportation of people; but, by this new grant, the adventurers of the northern colony had also utterly excluded those of the southern from fishing upon that coast, without their leave and license first sought and obtained, which was contrary and manifestly repugnant to that community and freedom which his Majesty, by the first patent, it is conceived, hath been pleased to grant unto the other colony.

"The court, therefore, knowing no reason why they should lose their former right granted unto them by the first patent, the sea also being to all as free and common as the air, and finding less reason why Sir Ferdinando Gorges should now appropriate and make a monopoly of the fishing, which hath already cost this company £6,000, the only means left (now the lotteries are almost spent and other supply begins to fail) to enable them to transport the people and sustain their plantation withal, did, with a general consent, resolve forthwith to petition to his Majesty for a redress herein, and to pray a further declaration of his gracious pleasure and intention concerning that clause of prohibition and restraint inserted in the new patent, whereby they were defeated of their liberty of fishing. Whereupon they appointed the committee to draw the said petition, and to make it, in substance, agreeable to those three points Sir Edwin Sandys had delivered in open court. And for that Sir Thomas Roe was the next day to go to the court, they desiring him to present the same to his Majesty."†

November 13, 1620.—"Sir Thomas Roe made now a report of his highness's gracious answer thereunto, who said that if anything were passed in New England patent that might be prejudicial to the southern colony, it was surrepti-

---

adventure nothing unless they went to Virginia, and those who were most relied on fell in utter dislike of Virginia, and would do nothing if they went thither.

"Howbeit the patent for the northern part of the country not being fully settled at that time, they resolved to adventure with the patent they had, intending for some place more southward than they fell upon, in the voyage at Cape Cod, as may appear afterwards."

Captain Jones, the navigator of the Mayflower, and John Peirce probably had arranged as to destination without the knowledge of the passengers.

* On the 18th of March, the company met at the capacious mansion of Sir Thomas Smith, in Philpot lane, when Sir Edwin Sandys reported that the committee had appeared before their lordships, and had there met Sir Ferdinando Gorges and others of the northern colony, and that their lordships, after listening to both sides, "pleased neither to allow nor disallow entirely, the one party or the other."

† The Virginia Company was looked upon by James as the nursery of a seditious parliament, while Gorges and others of the north colony were court favorites, and his Majesty granted the request of the latter, and, on July 23, directed a warrant which, on November 3, 1620, was, says Bancroft, issued to forty of his subjects, some of them members of his household and his government, the most wealthy and powerful of the English nobility, a patent which, in American annals, and even in the history of the world, has but one parallel. The adventurers and their successors were incorporated as "The Council established at Plymouth, in the county of Devon, for the planting, ruling, ordering, and governing of New England, in America."

tiously done, and that he had been abused thereby by those that pretended otherwise unto him. It pleased his Majesty to express as much, in effect, to my Lord of Southampton, with many other gracious words, in commendation of this plantation, and signified further that his Majesty forthwith gave commandment to my Lord Chancellor, then present, that if this new patent were not sealed for to forbear the seal, and if it were sealed and not delivered, that they should keep it in hand till they were better informed. His lordship further signified that upon Saturday last they had been with my Lord Chancellor about it, when were present the Duke of Lenox, the Earl of Arundel, Mr. Secretary, (Calvert,) and some others, who, after a full hearing of the allegations on both sides, did order that the patent should be delivered to be perused by some of the southern colony, who are to make report of what provisions they find thereunto at the next meeting." *

BALLOTING-BOX.

February 22, 1619, old style.—" Mr. Treasurer signified unto them of the balloting-box † standing upon the table, how it was intended at first another way as might appear by the arms upon it; but now Mr. Holloway had given it freely to this company, that therefore, to gratify him, they would entertain him into their Society by giving him a single share of land in Virginia, which being put to the question was ratified unto him; whereupon Mr. Deputy was entreated to provide a case for the better preserving of it.

ELECTION OF SECRETARY OF THE COLONY.

June 11, 1621.—Sir Edwin Sandys said, " But touching the secretary of state there, that now is, (Mr. Porey,‡) it remained to know their pleasure, whether

* Two days later the Earl of Southampton had another interview with the privy council, and signified that by a late conference with Sir Ferdinando Gorges they were now more in accord, "for that it was agreed upon both sides, for some important reasons, to renounce either of the patents, which was promised should be done by mutual advice of the counsel. Whereupon their lordships answered that, in the meanwhile, the patent of Sir Ferdinando Gorges should be sequestered and deposited in my Lord Chancellor's hands, according to his Majesty's express command."

† The London Athenæum of April 11, 1868, in an article on voting by the ballot-box, says: "Mr. John Bruce has turned up, within the last few days, a couple of papers which let us into the important secret of how and why the ballot-box was finally brought into use among us. It was not the first time, but it was the final time. It came to us from Holland in the bad days of Charles I; came in the year 1637."

The records of the Virginia Company show its use much earlier. It appears, however, from the same article, that King Charles ordered the discontinuance of the ballot-box. The order reads thus:

"AT HAMPTON COURT, *this 17th of September*, 1637.

"His Majesty this day sitting in council, taking into consideration the manifold inconveniences that may arise by the use of balloting-boxes, which is, of late, begun to be practiced by some corporations and companies, did declare his utter dislike thereof, and, with the advice of their lordships, ordered that no coporation nor company, either within the city of London and liberties, or elsewhere in this his Majesty's kingdom, shall use or permit to be used in any businesses whatever, any balloting-box, as they tender his Majesty's displeasure, and will answer the contrary at their peril.

"Whereof, as well the lord mayor of the city of London, for the time being, and all other mayors and head officers of corporations, as all governors, masters, and wardens of all companies in and about the cities of London and Westminster, and elsewhere, are to take notice and to see this his Majesty's pleasure and commandment duly observed."

‡ John Porey was a graduate of Cambridge, a great traveller and good writer, but gained the reputation of being a chronic tippler, and literary vagabond and sponger. A letter-writer on August 11, 1612, says: "It is long since I heard of Master Pory, but now at last understand he lies lieger at Paris, maintained by the Lord Carew."

Sir Dudley Carleton, wrote on July 9, 1613, from Venice: "Master Pory is come to Turin with purpose to see those parts, but wants *primum necessarium*, and hath, therefore, conjured me with these words—*by the kind and constant intelligence which passeth betwixt you and my best friends in England*—to send him fourteen doubloons, wherewith to disengage

they would continue him still in his said office or make a change. Whereupon it was signified that forasmuch as Mr. Porey had not carried himself well, in the said place, to the contentment of the company, it was considered to be the general purpose of the court to change him for a better, so near as they could, and therefore desired some others might be nominated unto them. Whereupon Mr. Deputy gave notice of four worthy gentlemen that had been recommended unto him for that place, all of them well-bred, sufficiently well qualified, so as the meanest of them seemed more worthy of a better place, not in respect of the quality thereof, but in respect of the entertainment belonging thereunto; so as it was his grief that they had not places for them all, but must be forced to dismiss three of them.

"The names of the said gentlemen were these: Mr. Paramore, Mr. Davison, Mr. Smith, and Waterhouse, who hath been recommended by Sir John Danvers for three things especially, namely, his honesty, religion, and sufficiency, for which he would undertake, upon that knowledge they had of him, this gentleman, Mr. Waterhouse, should make good to give full satisfaction.

"But it was signified that they all four having been recommended to the Lord of Southampton, his lordship was so nobly minded toward this company as to leave them to their free liberty of choice of any of them by an orderly election, and therefore wished they would, in the mean time, make some further inquiry against the next court."

June 13.—Mr. Deputy stated that there were four gentlemen proposed for the secretary's place, "being all of them recommended, by worthy persons, for their honesty, sufficiency, and experience in secretary affairs, but because no more but three could stand for the election, it was put to the question which three they would have nominated for that purpose, whereupon Mr. Smith* was dismissed, and the other three appointed to stand for the election, who being all three met to the balloting-box, choice was made of Mr. Davison, he having the majority of balls, who, being called in to take notice that the secretary's place was fallen upon him, did declare his thankful acknowledgments of their favor towards him, promising his best to answer their expectations of him."

---

him, where he lies in pawn, not knowing how to go forward or backward. I have done more in respect of his friends than himself, for I hear he is fallen too much in love with the pot to be much esteemed, and have sent him what he wrote for by Matthew, the post."

A correspondent of Carleton wrote on August 1 of the same year: "You had not need meet with many such poor moths as Master Pory, who must have both *meat* and *money*, for *drink* he will find out himself, if it be *above ground*, or no deeper than the *cellar*."

Sir Dudley Carleton, on August 22, 1617, writes from Hague to a friend: "If Mr. Porey have done with Constantinople, and can *Star Saldo* against the pot, which is hard in this country, he shall be welcome unto me, for I love an old acquaintance." After visiting Constantinople he was, for a brief period in 1617, an attaché of the English legation at the Hague, about the time of the residence there of the learned Puritan divine, Dr. William Ames, whose preaching the English Ambassador attended. In 1619 he was made secretary of the colony of Virginia, and after his recall, while returning to England, he stopped at the infant Plymouth settlement and had pleasant intercourse with Governor Bradford and Elder Brewster, with whom he may have been acquainted in Holland, and received from them some books, which he esteemed as "jewels," he says, in a note to Bradford dated August 28, 1622, and signed, "Your unfeigned and firm friend." (See Bradford's New Plymouth.)

A letter from London, dated July 26, 1623, says: "Our old acquaintance, Mr. Porey, is in poor case, and in prison at the Terceras, whither he was driven, by contrary winds, from the north coast of Virginia, where he had been upon some discovery, and upon his arrival was arraigned and in danger to be hanged for a pirate."

On his arrival in London he associated with the disaffected minority of the Virginia company, who succeeded in arousing the prejudices of the King so as to deprive them of the government of the colony.

In 1624 he was one of a commission appointed by order of James to proceed to Virginia and report upon its condition. At Jamestown he displayed a lack of honor in bribing Edward Sharpless, clerk of the council, to give him a copy of their proceedings, for which the perjured clerk was made by the Virginians to stand in the pillory and lose an ear.

* Captain John Smith.

HOMELESS BOYS AND GIRLS OF LONDON.

To the Right Honorable Sir Wm. Cockaine,* knight lord mayor of the city of London, and the right worthys the aldermen, his brethren, and the worthys the common council of the city:

The treasurer, council, and company of Virginia, assembled in their great and general court the 17th of November, 1619, have taken into consideration the continual great forwardness of this honourable city in advancing the plantation of Virginia, and particularly in furnishing out one hundred children this last year, which, by the goodness of God, have safely arrived (save such as died in the way) and are well pleased, we doubt not, for this benefit, for which, your bountiful assistance, we, in the name of the whole plantation, do yield unto you deserved thanks.

And forasmuch as we have now resolved to send this next spring very large supplies for the strength and increasing of the colony, styled by the name of the London colony, and find that the sending of these children to be apprenticed hath been very grateful to the people, we pray your lordship and the rest, pursuit of your former so precious actions, to renew the like favours, and furnish us again with one hundred more for the next spring.

Our desire is that we may have them of 12 years old and upward, with allowance of £3 apiece for their transportation, and 40*s.* apiece for their apparel, as was formerly granted. They shall be apprenticed; the boys till they come to 21 years of age; the girls till like age, or till they be married, and afterward they shall be placed as tenants upon the public lands, with best conditions, where they shall have houses with stock of corn and cattle to begin with, and afterward the moiety of all increase and profit whatsoever.

And so we leave this motion to your honourable and grave consideration.

COMPANION OF POCAHONTAS SICK IN LONDON.

May 11, 1620.—"The court taking notice from Sir William Throgmorton that one of the maidens which was brought over by Sir Thomas Dale† from

---

* William Cockaine was a distinguished merchant; sheriff in 1609; chief of the new company of merchant adventurers, which gave King James a great banquet on June 22, 1609, at his house, and there knighted. He died in 1626, and the distinguished poet and divine, John Donne, preached his funeral sermon.

The following letter of Sir Edwin Sandys on January 28, 1620, to one of the King's secretaries, Sir Robert Naunton, shows that the children were not always willing to embark.

"The city of London have appointed one hundred children from the superfluous multitude to be transported to Virginia, there to be bound apprentices upon very beneficial conditions. They have also granted £500 for their passage and outfit. Some of the ill-disposed children, who, under severe masters in Virginia, may be brought to goodness, and of whom the city is specially desirous to be disburdened, declare their unwillingness to go. The city wanting authority to deliver, and the Virginia Company to transport these children against their will, desire higher authority to get over the difficulty." (Cal. State Papers, Colonial Series.)

Another paper will throw some light on the abuses in this business.

"*Sir Edward Hext, Justice of the Peace of Somersetshire, to the Privy Council:*

"Upon complaint that Owen Evans, messenger of the Chamber, had a pretended commission to press maidens to be sent to Virginia and the Bermudas, and received money thereby, he issued a warrant for his apprehension. Evans' undue proceedings bred such terror to the poor maidens that 40 have fled from one parish to obscure places, and their parents do not know what has become of them."

† George, Lord Carew, writing in June, 1616, to Sir Thomas Roe, says: "Sir Thomas Dale returned from Virginia, brought divers men and women of that country to be educated in England."

Rev. William Gouge, D.D., educated at Cambridge, an eminent Puritan, was cousin of Rev. Alexander Whitaker, called by Bancroft the Apostle of Virginia, who came with Sir Thomas Dale, and in 1617 was drowned.

Gouge was noted for active benevolence, as well as for scholarship and pulpit oratory. In 1643 he was a member of the celebrated Westminster Assembly of Divines, and frequently occupied the moderator's chair. After a pastorate of forty-five years at Blackfriars, London, he died December 12, 1653, aged 79. When offered more profitable positions he always declined, saying that "his highest ambition was to go from Blackfriars to Heaven."

Virginia, a native of the country, who sometimes dwelt as a servant with a mercer in Cheapside, is now very weak of a consumption at Mr. Gouge's in the Blackfriars, who hath great care and taken great pains to comfort her both in soul and body; whereupon for her recovery the company are agreed to be at the charge of XX*s.* a week for three months, (if it please God she be not before the expiration thereof, restored to health or die in the mean season,) for the administering of physick and cordials for her health, and that the first payment begin this day seven-night, because Mr. Treasurer, for this year, reported his accounts were set up.

"Sir William Throgmorton, out of his private purse, promised to give XL*s.*, all which money is ordered to be paid to Mr. Gouge through the good assurance that the company hath of his careful management."

JOHN ROLFE AND POCAHONTAS.

April 30, 1621.—Sir John Danvers signified that it was the request of my lady Lawarre unto this court, that in consideration of her goods remaining in the hands of Mr. Rolfe * in Virginia, she might receive satisfaction for the same out of his tobacco now sent home.

But forasmuch as it is supposed the said tobacco is none of the said Rolfe's, but belonged to Mr. Peirce, it was thought fit that Mr. Henry Rolfe should acquaint my lady Lawarre † of his brother's offer to make her ladyship good and faithful account of all such goods as remain in his hands upon her lady's direction to that effect.

July 10, 1621.—"It was signified that the lady Lawarre desired the court would please to grant her a commission directed to Sir Francis Wyatt, Mr. George Sandys, and others, to examine and certify what goods and money of her late husband's, deceased, came to the hands of Mr. Rolfe in the year 1611, and to require the attending to his promise [that] she may be satisfied."

October 7, 1622.—"Mr. Henry Rolfe in his petition desiring the estate his brother John Rolfe, deceased, left in Virginia, might be enquired out for the maintenance of his relict wife and children, and for his indemnity, having brought up the child his said brother had by Powhatan's daughter,‡ is yet living and in his custody.

---

* John Rolfe and wife went to Virginia in the expedition that sailed in 1609 from England, and while detained at Bermuda, where the ships had been stranded in a storm, he became the father of a child, who was christened Bermuda Rolfe by Chaplain Buck.

Strachey, secretary of Lord De Lawarre, says, "The 11th of February [1610, old style] we had a child of one John Rolfe christened, of which Captain Newport and myself were witnesses." (Purchas, volume 4, p. 1744.)

† She was the widow of Thomas, third Lord Delaware, captain-general of all the provinces in Virginia. He had been dead for more than two years. A letter written from London, October 5, 1618, says: "This day news arrived of my Lord de la War's death in his voyage to Virginia."

‡ Strachey, who was Secretary of the colony from May, 1610, for a period of about two years, in his Historie of Travaile, published by the Hakluyt Society, several times alludes to Powhatan's daughter. In book 1, page 54, he remarks: "I say they often reported to us that Powhatan had then living twenty sons and ten daughters, * * * besides Pocohunta, a daughter of his, using sometime to our fort in times past, now married to a private captain called Kocoum some two years since."

On page 132 of the same book he says: "The younger women go not shadowed amongst their own company until they be nigh eleven or twelve returns of the leaf old, nor are they much ashamed thereof, and therefore would the before-remembered Pochahuntas, a well featured but wanton young girl, Powhatan's daughter, sometimes resorting to our fort, of the age then of eleven or twelve years, get the boys forth with her into the market place and make them wheel, falling on their hands, turning up their heels upwards, whom she would follow and wheel so herself, naked as she was, all the fort over."

On another page he writes: "The great King Powhatan called a young daughter of his, whom he loved well, Pochahuntas, which may signify little wanton, howbeit she was rightly called Amonate at more ripe years."

There appears to have been an effort to build up a fifth kingdom and an Anglo-Indian

It was ordered that the governor and council of Virginia should cause inquiries to be what lands and goods the said John Rolfe died seized of; and in case it be found the said Rolfe made no will, then to take such order for the petitioner's indemnity, and for the maintenance of the said children and his relict wife as they shall find his estate will bear, (his debt unto the company and others being first satisfied,) and to return unto the company an account of their proceedings."

CAPTAIN JOHN SMITH PROPOSES TO COMPILE A HISTORY.

April 12, 1621.—"Mr. Smith moved, that forasmuch as lotteries were now suspended, which hath unto now contributed the real and substantial food by which Virginia hath been nourished, that instead thereof she might be now preserved by divulging fair and good report as she and her worthy undertakers did well deserve, declaring that it would not but much advance the plantation in the popular opinion of the common subject to have a fair and conspicuous history compiled of that country from the first discovery to this day, and to have the memory and fame of many of their worthies, though they be dead, to live and be transmitted to all posterity, as namely: Sir Thomas Dale, Sir George Somers, Sir Walter Raleigh, the Lord De-la-warr, Sir Thomas Gates, and divers others,* whereunto, were it not for suspicions of flattery, he would write also the

---

nobility in Virginia by a few adventurers. On September 22, 1612, the Spanish ambassador, De Cunega, writes to his King: "Although some suppose the plantation to decrease, he is credibly informed that there is a determination to marry some of the people that go over to the Virginians; forty or fifty are already so married, and English women intermingle and are received kindly by the natives. A zealous minister has been wounded for reprehending it." (Cal. State Papers, colonial, 1584–1660.)

The Virginia Company on August 23, 1618, wrote to the crafty Governor Argall: "We cannot imagine why you should give us warning that Opechankano and the natives have given the country to Mr. Rolfe's child, and that they reserve it from all others till he comes of years, except, as we suppose, as some do here report it, to be a device of your own, to some special purpose for yourself."

* It is noteworthy that Smith does not allude to Captain Christopher Newport, the commander of the first expedition to Virginia, with whom he had sailed and was closely associated during the first and second visits of that experienced mariner to Jamestown.

Thomas Fuller, who was a young man when Smith died, thus describes him in the "Worthies of England:"

"John Smith, captain, was born in this county, [Cheshire,] as Master Arthur Smith, his kinsman and my schoolmaster, did inform me. * * * From the Turks in Europe he passed to the pagans in America, where such his perils, preservations, dangers, deliverances, they seem to most men *above belief*, to some *beyond truth*. Yet have we two witnesses to attest them, the prose and the pictures, *both in his own book*, and it soundeth much to the diminution of his deeds that he *alone* is the herald to publish and proclaim them. * * * * He led his old age in London, where his having a prince's mind imprisoned in a poor man's purse, rendered him to the contempt of such who were not ingenuous. Yet he efforted his spirits with the remembrance and relation of what formerly he had been and what he had done. He was buried in Sepulchre's Church choir, on the south side thereof, having a ranting epitaph inscribed in a table over him, too long to transcribe. Only we will insert the first and last verses, the rather because one may fit Alexander's life for his valour, and the other his death for his religion:

'Here lies one conquered, who hath conquered kings.'
'O! may his soul in Elysium sleep.'

"The orthography, poetry, history, and divinity in this epitaph are much alike. He died on the 21st of June, 1631."

As he is said to have been born in 1579, he lived fifry-two years. As the French travellers in America, Hennepin and La Hontan, fascinated by their bold misstatements, so did John Smith. In a letter written from Jamestown, in October, 1609, to Cecil, Earl of Salisbury, is the following statement:

"Captain John Smith, president, who reigned sole governor, and is now sent home to *answer some misdemeanors*." (Cal. State Papers, colonial, 1574–1660.)

Wingfield, first president of the Virginia colony, in a "Discourse of Virginia," printed from the manuscripts in Lambeth library, in volume 4, Coll. Am. Ant. Society, asserts that "Mr. Smyth, in the time of our hunger, had spread a rumor in the colony that I did feast myself and my servants out of the common store, with intent, as I gathered, to have stirred the dis-

name of many other worthies now living; and some of them now present in court might have also their honorable and good deserving recommended to eternal thankfulness, for our inabilities had, as yet, no other coin wherewith to recompense their pains and merit; affirming, also, that the best now planted parts of America which the Spanish government, in their annals or their histories of those times in their like age of ours, (now twelve years old,) in Virginia, afforded better matter of relation than Virginia hath done and doth. With what effect such a general history, deduced to the life to this year, would work throughout the kingdom, with the general and common subjects, may be gathered by the little pamphlets * or declarations lately printed. And, besides, few succeeding years would soon consume the lives of many whose living memories yet retained much, and devour those letters and intelligences which yet remain in loose and neglected papers, for which boldness, in moving thereof, he prayed his lordship's pardon, led thereunto by some of his fellows of the generality."

NAVIGATION PROPOSED.

March 18, 1619, old style.—Sir Edwin Sandys "also signified that Sir George Yeardley desired of them, for the good of the colony, that a navigation might be set up which would produce good benefit to the plantation, and, to that end, nominated unto them one Marmaduke Rayner,† who is willing to go, if they please to give him his passage, which man being also well known to Sir Thomas Roe, he gave very good commendations of him, whereupon it was agreed, upon the terms mentioned, he should be sent."

PROPOSED SETTLEMENT IN NORTH CAROLINA.

November 15, 1620.—"Some of the Somers Island Company moved that the court would be pleased, as well in respect that the Bermudas was sold unto them

contented company against me. I told him privately, in Mr. Gosnold's tent, that indeed I had caused a half pint of peas to be sodden with a piece of pork of my own provision, for a poor old man, which, in a sickness whereof he died, he much desired, and said, that if out of his malice he had given it out otherwise, he did tell a lie. It was proved to his face that he begged in Ireland like a rogue without a license. * * * * Mr. Smythe's quarrel to me was because his name was mentioned in the intended and confessed mutiny by Galthropp."

* The first pamphlet relative to the colony of Virginia was published in 1608, with the following title:

"A Trve Relation of such occurrences and accidents of noate as hath hapened in Virginia since the first planting of that collony, which is now resident in the South part thereof, till the last returne from thence. Written by Captaine Smith, coronell of the said collony, to a worshipfull friend of his in England. London. Printed for John Tappe, and are to bee solde at the Greyhound in Paules Church-yard, by W. W. 1608."

This work, carefully edited by Mr. Charles Deane, was reproduced in 1866, by Wiggin & Lunt, of Boston.

In his first book on Virginia, Smith says not one word relative to his rescue from death by Pocahontas. After speaking of Powhatan's desire that he should come and live with him, he adds: "This request I promised to performe; and thus, having with all the kindnes hee could dessire, sought to content mee, hee sent me home with 4 men, one that usually carried my Gowne and Knapsacke after me, two other loded with bread, and one to accompanie me." (Deane's edition of True Relation, p. 38.)

Fifteen years after his return to England he published the "General History," and in this Powhatan is transformed to a savage wretch, with his minions dragging the valiant captain toward two great stones in front of the Indian king, and being ready with their clubs to beat out his brains, Pocahontas, the king's dearest daughter, when no entreaty could prevail, got his head into her arms and laid her own upon his to save him from death."

Mr. Deane clearly points out the embellishments and contradictions in his last work, giving "to the narrative an air of romance."

Palfrey says Smith "travelled about the south and west of England distributing books and maps;" (History of N. England, volume 1, p. 95,) and in a note remarks: "I presume I am not the first reader who has been haunted by incredulity respecting some of the adventures of Smith." (Volume 1, p. 89.)

† The following summer Rayner made three voyages to North Carolina, and in 1627 was master of the ship Temperance, which sailed from Virginia to London.

for a far greater quantity of land than they now find it to be, as also for the better enabling of them to subsist and procure and maintain a mutual dependence and traffic hereafter, to grant and confirm unto them, in this great and general quarter court, a good portion of land in Virginia, on that side of the coast as lies nearest unto them, either at Ronoque southerly, or else whereat shall be most convenient for them, not being yet inhabited; which request the court taking into consideration, did order and agree, that according to the number of their shares, being in all 400 or thereabouts, they should have for every share 100 acres of land in Virginia, and fifty acres for every person that shall be transported thither. * * * * The court ordered that a letter should be written to the governor to set out their bounds and limits where they shall like best to seat themselves, so as they may not be prejudicial to any other plantation there already."

DISCOVERIES OF RAYNER, SAVAGE, AND DERMER.

July 10, 1621.—"There was also read unto the company a relation of three several voyages, made this last summer, unto the southward to Roanocke, made by Mr. Marmaduke Rayner; a second by Ensign Savadge * in the great bay, wherein is a great trade of furs by Frenchmen; a third, Mr. Dirmer s discovery from Cape Charles to Cape Codd, up Delaware river and Hudson's river, being but twenty or thirty leagues from our plantation, and within our limits, in which rivers were found divers ships of Amsterdam and Horn, who yearly had there a great and rich trade for furs, which have moved the governor and council of state in Virginia earnestly to solicit and invite the company to undertake so certain and gainful a voyage."

* Purchas (volume 4, p. 1784) gives the credit of this discovery to Pory. His words are: "Master John Porie hath of late made a discovery into the great bay northward, * * where are now settled near one hundred English very happily, with hope of a very good trade in furs there to be had."

This was probably the commencement of the settlement of Kent island in Chesapeake bay. As early as 1613, Argall sailed with Sir Thomas Dale up this bay, and in a letter predicted that they could "find a safe passage for boats and barges thither by a cut out of the bottom of the bay into the Delaware bay." (Purchas, volume 4, p. 1764.)

www.ingramcontent.com/pod-product-compliance
Lightning Source LLC
LaVergne TN
LVHW011148110826
845150LV00008B/2568